A
Betty Crocker
PICTURE COOKBOOK
Stews and Soups
and Go-With Breads

 GOLDEN PRESS/NEW YORK
Western Publishing Company, Inc.
Racine, Wisconsin

Library of Congress Catalog Card Number: 81-83382
ISBN 0-307-09669-6

CONTENTS

Breads

Cut beef into 2-inch pieces.

Cut carrots into ½-inch slices.

Savory Beef Ragout

1½ pounds beef chuck or bottom round, cut
   into 2-inch pieces
 2 tablespoons vegetable oil
 ¼ cup all-purpose flour
 2 cups water
 1 can (about 8½ ounces) stewed tomatoes
 3 sprigs parsley
 2 teaspoons salt
 ½ teaspoon dried thyme leaves
 ¼ teaspoon dried sage leaves
 ¼ teaspoon pepper
 1 bay leaf
 1 clove garlic, finely chopped
 6 small onions
 3 large carrots, cut diagonally into ½-inch
   slices (about 2 cups)
 1 package (10 ounces) frozen lima beans,
   broken apart

Brown beef pieces in oil in Dutch oven; remove beef. Drain fat from Dutch oven, reserving 2 tablespoons. Return 2 tablespoons fat to Dutch oven. (If necessary, add enough oil to measure 2 tablespoons.)

Stir in flour. Cook and stir over low heat until smooth and bubbly; remove from heat. Add water. Heat to boiling, stirring constantly. Stir in beef, tomatoes, parsley, salt, thyme, sage, pepper, bay leaf and garlic. Heat to boiling; reduce heat. Cover and simmer 1 hour.

Add onions and carrots. Cover and simmer until beef and vegetables are tender, 40 to 50 minutes. Stir in frozen beans. Cover and simmer until beans are tender, about 10 minutes.   6 SERVINGS.

Remove bacon with tongs; drain on paper towels.

Cut 1 pound Polish sausage into ½-inch slices.

Use a knife to shred cabbage coarsely and evenly.

Cut apples into fourths; core and then slice.

Beef and Sausage Stew

4 slices bacon
1 pound beef stew meat, cut into 1-inch
  pieces
1 large onion, sliced
2 cups water
1 can (12 ounces) beer
2 teaspoons instant beef bouillon
1 teaspoon salt
½ teaspoon dried thyme leaves
¼ teaspoon pepper
2 whole cloves
1 bay leaf
3 medium carrots, cut diagonally into ½-inch
  slices (about 1½ cups)
1 pound Polish sausage, cut into ½-inch
  slices
4 ounces uncooked noodles (about 2 cups)
½ medium head cabbage, coarsely shredded
  (about 2 cups)
2 medium apples, sliced

Fry bacon slices in Dutch oven over medium heat until crisp; remove bacon and drain on paper towels. Brown beef stew meat in bacon fat; push beef to side. Cook and stir onion in bacon fat until tender; drain. Stir in water, beer, instant bouillon, salt, thyme, pepper, cloves and bay leaf. Heat to boiling; reduce heat. Cover and simmer 1 hour.

Add carrots and sausage. Heat to boiling; reduce heat. Cover and simmer 30 minutes.

Crumble bacon; stir bacon, noodles, cabbage and apples into stew. Heat to boiling; reduce heat. Cover and simmer until noodles are tender, 10 to 15 minutes.   6 TO 8 SERVINGS.

Good Beef Stew

2 pounds beef stew meat, cut into 1-inch pieces
⅓ cup all-purpose flour
¼ cup vegetable oil
½ cup snipped parsley
3 tablespoons packed brown sugar
1 tablespoon salt
½ teaspoon dried rosemary leaves
1 can (10½ ounces) condensed beef broth
¼ cup vinegar
1 can (12 ounces) beer
1 large onion, sliced
1 small clove garlic, crushed
6 large potatoes

Heat oven to 325°. Coat beef pieces with flour. Brown beef, a few pieces at a time, in oil in Dutch oven over medium heat; drain. Remove beef from Dutch oven.

Mix parsley, brown sugar, salt and rosemary in Dutch oven. Stir in broth and vinegar gradually, scraping bottom of pan, until gravy is smooth. Heat to boiling, stirring constantly. Stir in beer, onion, garlic and beef. Add potatoes. Cover and bake until beef and potatoes are tender, about 3 hours.   6 SERVINGS.

BEEF STEW MEAT is usually cut from the boneless chuck sections (shoulder cut, pictured top, arm or blade cuts) or round section (round cut, pictured bottom, or rump cut). If you compare the price per pound of these cuts with the price of ready-cut beef stew meat, you may find it more economical to cut up your own beef.

Two-Time Beef Stew

⅓ cup all-purpose flour
1 teaspoon salt
¼ teaspoon pepper
2 pounds beef stew meat, cut into 1-inch
  pieces
2 tablespoons vegetable oil
1 can (16 ounces) stewed tomatoes
2 cups water
2 teaspoons salt
2 teaspoons instant beef bouillon
1 bay leaf

Mix flour, 1 teaspoon salt and the pepper. Coat beef stew pieces with flour mixture. Brown beef in oil in Dutch oven. Stir in tomatoes, water, 2 teaspoons salt, the instant bouillon and bay leaf. Heat to boiling; reduce heat. Cover and simmer until beef is tender, 1 to 1½ hours. Divide beef mixture between two 1-quart freezer containers. Cool quickly. Cover and label; freeze up to 3 months.

■**45 minutes before serving,** dip 1 container into hot water to loosen. Place frozen beef and ½ cup water in Dutch oven. Cover and heat over medium heat, turning block occasionally, until thawed, about 15 minutes. Add 1 package (10 ounces) frozen lima beans and 2 medium onions, cut into fourths. Cover and simmer until lima beans are tender, about 15 minutes.   4 SERVINGS.

■**45 minutes before serving,** dip 1 container into hot water to loosen. Place frozen beef, 2 medium carrots, thinly sliced, and ¾ cup water in Dutch oven. Cover and heat over medium heat, turning occasionally, until thawed, 20 minutes; add 1 package (10 ounces) frozen Brussels sprouts. Cover and simmer until carrots and Brussels sprouts are tender, about 15 minutes.   4 SERVINGS.

Bean Stew

1 cup great northern beans
1 tablespoon vegetable oil
2 cups water
1 pound beef stew meat, cut into 1-inch
  pieces
1 pound pork stew meat, cut into 1-inch
  pieces
1 large onion, sliced
3 tablespoons vegetable oil
3 medium carrots, cut into ½-inch slices
1 tablespoon plus 1 teaspoon paprika
1½ teaspoons salt
½ teaspoon cayenne red pepper
¼ teaspoon pepper
1 can (6 ounces) tomato paste
1 package (10 ounces) frozen Brussels
  sprouts, partially thawed
1 can (8 ounces) whole kernel corn

Heat beans, 1 tablespoon oil and water to boiling; boil 2 minutes. Remove from heat. Cover and let stand while preparing meat and onion.

Cook and stir beef and pork stew meat and onion in 3 tablespoons oil in Dutch oven until onion is tender, about 5 minutes. Stir in beans (with water), carrots, paprika, salt, red pepper and pepper. Heat to boiling; reduce heat. Simmer uncovered until meat is tender, 1½ to 2 hours.

Stir tomato paste, Brussels sprouts and corn (with liquid) into meat mixture. Simmer uncovered until Brussels sprouts are tender, about 15 minutes.   8 SERVINGS.

Based on *Bredi,* a richly flavored mutton stew.

Heat beans, oil and water to boiling; boil 2 minutes.

Cover and let stand while preparing meat and onion.

Stir beans (with water), carrots, seasonings into meat.

After meat is tender, add the Brussels sprouts and corn.

Trim any excess fat from the beef short ribs.

Brown ribs over medium heat, turning with tongs.

Short Rib Stew

---

  3 pounds beef short ribs
1½ cups water
  2 medium onions, sliced
  2 tablespoons vinegar or lemon juice
  2 teaspoons salt
  ¼ teaspoon pepper
  2 bay leaves
  1 package (10 ounces) frozen lima beans
  4 medium carrots, cut into 3x½-inch strips
  1 tablespoon packed brown sugar
  ¼ teaspoon ground ginger
    Gravy (right)

Trim excess fat from beef short ribs. Brown beef in 12-inch skillet; drain. Add water, onions, vinegar, salt, pepper and bay leaves. Heat to boiling; reduce heat. Cover and simmer 1 hour.

Add frozen beans, carrots, brown sugar and ginger. Heat to boiling; reduce heat. Cover and simmer until vegetables are tender, about 45 minutes. Remove beef and vegetables to platter; keep warm. Prepare Gravy; serve with short ribs.　4 SERVINGS.

GRAVY

1½ cups beef broth
⅓ cup cold water
3 tablespoons flour

Skim excess fat from beef broth. Measure broth; if necessary, add enough water to measure 1½ cups. Return broth to Dutch oven. Shake water and flour in covered container. Stir flour mixture slowly into broth. Heat to boiling, stirring constantly. Boil and stir 1 minute.

Timing Tip: If you want to serve at different times, Short Rib Stew will hold covered over low heat up to 1 hour. Prepare Gravy just before serving.

Oxtail Stew

---

   3 tablespoons flour
   2 teaspoons dry mustard
   1 teaspoon salt
  ½ teaspoon chili powder
  ¼ teaspoon pepper
2½ pounds oxtails, cut into 2-inch pieces
   1 medium onion, coarsely chopped (about
      ½ cup)
  ¼ cup vegetable oil
   2 cans (16 ounces each) stewed tomatoes
   1 can (15 ounces) tomato sauce
   1 cup water
   1 teaspoon Worcestershire sauce
   1 bay leaf
  ½ teaspoon dried thyme leaves
   2 medium stalks celery, sliced
   1 package (10 ounces) frozen whole okra,
      partially thawed
     Hot cooked rice

Mix flour, mustard, salt, chili powder and pepper. Coat oxtails with flour mixture. Cook and turn oxtails and onion in oil in 4-quart Dutch oven until oxtails are brown on all sides; drain.

Stir in tomatoes, tomato sauce, water, Worcestershire sauce, bay leaf and thyme. Heat to boiling; reduce heat. Cover and simmer until oxtails are tender, about 3 hours. Refrigerate several hours; skim off fat.

Stir celery and okra into oxtail mixture. Heat to boiling; reduce heat. Cover and simmer until okra is tender, about 15 minutes. Serve with rice.   6 SERVINGS.

Based on the thrifty stews traditional in rural England.

Coat oxtails with mixture of flour and dry seasonings.

Cook and turn the oxtails and onion in oil, then drain.

Stir in tomatoes, tomato sauce, water, Worcestershire sauce, the bay leaf and thyme.

Before serving, stir celery and okra into oxtail mixture. Simmer until okra is tender.

To make light dumplings, cook uncovered 10 minutes.

Cover the dumplings and cook them 10 minutes longer.

Stew with Ginger Dumplings

1 can (40 ounces) beef stew
1 can (16 ounces) chow mein vegetables, drained
1 can (8 ounces) water chestnuts, drained and cut in half
½ cup broken pecans
1 to 1½ teaspoons soy sauce
½ teaspoon ground ginger
1 cup biscuit baking mix
⅓ cup milk
¼ teaspoon ground ginger

Mix stew, chow mein vegetables, water chestnuts, pecans, soy sauce and ½ teaspoon ginger in 10-inch skillet. Heat to boiling over medium heat, stirring occasionally.

Stir baking mix, milk and ¼ teaspoon ginger until a soft dough forms. Drop dough by small spoonfuls onto boiling stew; reduce heat. Cook uncovered 10 minutes. Cover and cook 10 minutes longer.   6 TO 8 SERVINGS.

SHELF SENSE

Canned foods retain many vitamins and minerals due to timely harvesting and swift processing. To save those carefully guarded nutrients, heat the shortest possible time. Do not overcook. All heat-processed canned foods (except bacon) are thoroughly cooked during processing and are ready to eat from the can.

PORK STEW MEAT is usually cut from the Boston shoulder section (Boston roast slice, pictured top, or blade steak, pictured bottom) or picnic shoulder section (arm picnic or arm steak cuts). Compare price per pound of these cuts with ready-cut pork stew meat; you may prefer to cut up your own pork for stews.

Pork-Kraut Stew

- 2 pounds pork stew meat, cut into 1-inch pieces
- 2 tablespoons vegetable oil
- 2 medium onions, chopped (about 1 cup)
- 1 clove garlic, finely chopped
- 2 cups water
- 1 tablespoon paprika
- 2 teaspoons instant chicken bouillon
- 1½ teaspoons caraway seed
- 1 teaspoon salt
- ⅛ teaspoon pepper
- 1 can (27 ounces) sauerkraut, drained
  Snipped parsley
- 1 carton (8 ounces) dairy sour cream

Cook and stir pork stew meat in oil in 10-inch skillet over medium heat until pork is brown; drain on paper towels. Cook and stir onions and garlic in same skillet until onions are tender. Stir in pork, water, paprika, instant bouillon, caraway seed, salt and pepper. Heat to boiling; reduce heat. Cover and simmer 1 hour.

Stir sauerkraut into pork mixture. Heat to boiling; reduce heat. Cover and simmer until pork is tender, about 30 minutes. Sprinkle with parsley and serve with sour cream. 6 TO 8 SERVINGS.

Hungarian Holiday Stew: Stir a mixture of ¼ cup water and 2 tablespoons flour into pork mixture after second simmering. Heat to boiling, stirring constantly. Boil and stir 1 minute; reduce heat. Stir in sour cream; heat just until mixture is hot. Sprinkle with parsley.

From Hungary, and in the tradition of *Gulyás.*

DILL is an attractive feathery herb with a pungent aroma. The seeds are often used in coleslaw, sauerkraut and pickling. The leaves add both color and flavor to stews, sauces, vegetables, cottage cheese and salads. Dried leaves are marketed as dill weed. 1 teaspoon dried leaves equals 1 tablespoon fresh.

Country-Style Pork Dinner

2½ pounds pork boneless Boston shoulder
  4 medium carrots, halved lengthwise and
     cut into 2-inch pieces
1¼ cups hot water
  2 teaspoons instant chicken bouillon
  1 teaspoon dried dill weed
  1 teaspoon onion salt
  ¼ teaspoon pepper
  1 package (10 ounces) frozen Brussels
     sprouts
  1 package (10 ounces) frozen cauliflower
  ½ teaspoon salt

Trim excess fat from pork shoulder; cut pork into 1-inch pieces. Rub 10-inch skillet with fat cut from pork. Brown pork pieces in skillet. Stir in carrots, water, instant bouillon, dill, onion salt and pepper. Heat to boiling; reduce heat. Cover and simmer 1 hour.

Rinse frozen Brussels sprouts and cauliflower under running cold water to separate. Stir Brussels sprouts and cauliflower into pork mixture; sprinkle with salt. Heat to boiling; reduce heat. Cover and simmer until vegetables are tender, 15 to 20 minutes.   6 SERVINGS.

Place browned lamb on onions and carrots in Dutch oven.

Pour on wine mixture; stir 'n beans. Cover and simmer.

Lamb and Bean Stew

½ pound dry white beans (about 1¼ cups)
3 medium onions, thinly sliced
3 medium carrots, cut into 1-inch pieces
¼ cup butter or margarine
2 pounds lamb stew meat, cut into 1-inch pieces
1 clove garlic, finely chopped
¼ cup vegetable oil
¾ cup dry white wine
1 cup boiling water
1 teaspoon instant chicken bouillon
2 medium tomatoes, peeled and chopped
1 teaspoon dried thyme leaves
2½ teaspoons salt
⅛ teaspoon pepper
1 bouquet garni

Place beans in 3-quart saucepan. Add water to 1 inch above beans. Heat to boiling; boil 2 minutes. Remove from heat; cover and let stand 1 hour. Drain.

Cook and stir onions and carrots in butter in Dutch oven over low heat, stirring occasionally, about 10 minutes.

Cook and stir lamb and garlic in oil in 10-inch skillet over medium heat until lamb is light brown. Remove lamb, reserving pan juices. Place lamb on onions and carrots in Dutch oven. Stir wine into reserved pan juices. Heat to boiling; boil and stir 2 minutes. Stir in remaining ingredients. Heat to boiling; pour on lamb in Dutch oven. Stir in beans. Heat to boiling; reduce heat. Cover and simmer until beans are tender, about 1½ hours. Refrigerate several hours. Skim off fat; reheat to serve.   4 TO 6 SERVINGS.

Remove the cooked and cooled chicken meat from the bones, then cut into bite-size pieces.

Add vegetables, rice and red pepper sauce to Dutch oven; break up tomatoes with fork.

Chicken Gumbo

3½-pound broiler-fryer chicken, cut up
2 cups water
2 teaspoons salt
1 clove garlic, finely chopped
1 large bay leaf, crumbled
2 large stalks celery (with leaves), cut
    diagonally into slices (about 1½ cups)
1 medium onion, chopped (about ½ cup)
1 can (28 ounces) whole tomatoes
1 package (10 ounces) frozen okra
1 can (7 ounces) whole kernel corn
⅓ cup uncooked regular rice
½ teaspoon red pepper sauce

Heat chicken pieces, water, salt, garlic and bay leaf to boiling in Dutch oven; reduce heat. Cover and simmer until chicken is done, about 45 minutes.

Remove chicken from broth; strain broth. Refrigerate chicken and broth. When cool, remove chicken from bones (skin can be removed if desired). Cut chicken into bite-size pieces. Skim excess fat from broth and place broth and chicken in Dutch oven. Stir in celery, onion, tomatoes (with liquid), frozen okra, corn (with liquid), rice and pepper sauce; break up tomatoes with fork. Heat to boiling; reduce heat. Cover and simmer until okra and rice are tender, 20 to 30 minutes. Garnish with snipped parsley. 8 SERVINGS.

Timing Tip: If you want to serve at different times, Chicken Gumbo will hold covered over low heat up to 1 hour.

Chicken Fricassee

---

     2 medium carrots, thinly sliced
     1 medium onion, thinly sliced
     6 tablespoons butter or margarine
     3-pound broiler-fryer chicken, cut up
     ½ teaspoon salt
     2 cans (10¾ ounces each) condensed
           chicken broth
     1 cup dry white wine or dry vermouth
     2 bouquets garnis (see note)
    16 small white onions
     ½ pound mushrooms, sliced
     1 tablespoon lemon juice
     2 egg yolks
     ½ cup whipping cream

Cook and stir carrots and onion slices in 4 tablespoons of
the butter in Dutch oven; push aside. Add chicken; cook
until golden, about 5 minutes. Add salt, broth, ½ cup wine
and 1 bouquet garni. Heat to boiling; reduce heat. Cover;
simmer until done, about 40 minutes.

Heat 16 onions and the remaining butter, wine and bouquet garni to boiling; reduce heat. Cover; simmer until onions are tender, 20 to 25 minutes. Remove onions and chicken pieces to warm platter with slotted spoon. Strain chicken broth and onion liquid together, discarding carrots and onion slices. Skim fat from broth. Heat broth, mushrooms and lemon juice to boiling; reduce to 2½ cups.

Mix egg yolks and cream. Beat 1 cup hot broth by tablespoonfuls into cream mixture. Beat in remaining broth. Heat to boiling, stirring constantly. Boil and stir 1 minute; pour on chicken and onions.   4 SERVINGS.

Note: For each bouquet garni, tie 2 sprigs parsley, ⅓ bay leaf and ⅛ teaspoon dried rosemary leaves in cheesecloth.

An American translation of *Fricassee de Poulet.*

Simmer the chicken with the carrots, onion, salt, broth, wine and 1 bouquet garni.

Heat onions, remaining butter, wine and bouquet garni to boiling; cover and simmer.

Cook strained broth mixture, mushrooms and lemon juice until reduced to 2½ cups.

Beat 1 cup broth by tablespoonfuls into cream mixture; beat in remaining broth.

Trim excess fat from beef cross rib pot roast.

Separate cauliflower into bite-size cauliflowerets.

Cut potatoes lengthwise into ¼-inch strips.

Cut up spinach easily with kitchen shears.

Garden Vegetable Soup

2- to 2½-pound beef cross rib pot roast
2½ cups water
2 teaspoons salt
1 teaspoon lemon juice
½ teaspoon dried basil leaves
¼ teaspoon pepper
2 beef bouillon cubes
1 bay leaf, crumbled
1 medium onion, chopped (about ½ cup)
1 can (16 ounces) stewed tomatoes
2 medium stalks celery (with leaves), cut into ½-inch slices (about 2 cups)
3 medium carrots, cut into ¼-inch slices (about 1½ cups)
1 cup cauliflowerets
½ cup sliced fresh mushrooms*
4 medium potatoes, cut lengthwise into ¼-inch strips
2 ounces fresh spinach or kale, cut up (about 1 cup)

Trim excess fat from beef pot roast. Cut beef into 1½-inch pieces; reserve bone. Brown beef pieces and bone in Dutch oven; drain. Stir in water, salt, lemon juice, basil, pepper, bouillon cubes, bay leaf and onion. Heat to boiling; reduce heat. Cover and simmer 1½ hours.

Stir in tomatoes, celery, carrots, cauliflowerets and mushrooms. Heat to boiling; reduce heat. Cover and simmer until beef is tender, about 40 minutes. Stir in potatoes. Cover and simmer until potatoes are tender, about 15 minutes. Sprinkle soup with spinach. Cover and simmer 5 minutes.   6 TO 8 SERVINGS.

*1 can (2 ounces) mushroom stems and pieces (with liquid) can be substituted for the fresh mushrooms.

BARLEY, one of the first known cereal grains to be cultivated, is nutritious and nutlike in flavor. It is used in soups, stews and casseroles or served as a side dish in place of rice or potatoes. It is available in both regular and quick-cooking forms, both of which can be stored in a cool, dry place on the cupboard shelf.

Beef and Barley Soup

    5 slices bacon
  1-pound beef chuck roast or steak, cut into
      1-inch pieces
    2 large onions, chopped (about 2 cups)
    2 cloves garlic, finely chopped
    2 cans (10½ ounces each) condensed beef
      broth
    2 cups water
   ¼ cup regular barley
 1½ teaspoons paprika
    1 teaspoon salt
   ¼ teaspoon caraway seed
   ⅛ teaspoon dried marjoram leaves
    3 medium potatoes, cut into ½-inch pieces
    2 medium carrots, sliced (about 1 cup)
    2 medium stalks celery, sliced
    1 can (16 ounces) stewed tomatoes
    1 package (10 ounces) frozen green peas,
      broken apart
    1 can (4 ounces) mushroom stems and
      pieces

Fry bacon in Dutch oven over medium heat until crisp; remove bacon and drain on paper towel. Cook and stir beef pieces, onions and garlic in bacon fat in Dutch oven until beef is brown. Stir in broth, water, barley, paprika, salt, caraway seed and marjoram. Heat to boiling; reduce heat. Cover and simmer 1½ hours.

Stir in potatoes, carrots, celery, tomatoes, frozen peas and mushrooms (with liquid). Heat to boiling; reduce heat. Cover and simmer until vegetables are tender, 30 to 40 minutes. Crumble bacon; sprinkle over soup.   8 SERVINGS.

Timing Tip: If you want to serve at different times, Beef and Barley Soup will hold covered over low heat up to 1 hour.

THYME is used to flavor meat, poultry, soups, stews and seafood. If you have sunshine in your kitchen window, thyme will grow through the winter. ¼ teaspoon dried is equal to 1 teaspoon fresh.

SWEET MARJORAM delicately accents sausages, stuffings, soups, stews, eggs, tomatoes, meats and fish. Rub the dried leaves between your fingers before using. ½ teaspoon dried is equal to 1 teaspoon fresh.

Easy Three-Bean Beef Soup

1 pound beef cubed steaks, cut into 1-inch
  pieces
2 tablespoons butter or margarine
1 can (28 ounces) whole tomatoes
1 can (10¾ ounces) condensed beef
  consommé
1 cup water
½ cup regular barley
¼ cup frozen chopped onion
1½ teaspoons salt
¼ teaspoon dried marjoram leaves
¼ teaspoon dried thyme leaves
1 package (10 ounces) frozen baby lima
  beans, broken apart
1 package (9 ounces) frozen Italian or
  French-style green beans, broken apart
1 can (15 ounces) butter beans, drained
¼ cup grated Romano cheese

Brown beef cubed steak pieces in butter in Dutch oven over medium heat. Stir in tomatoes (with liquid), consommé, water, barley, onion, salt, marjoram and thyme. Heat to boiling; reduce heat. Cover and simmer 50 minutes.

Stir in lima beans and green beans. Heat to boiling; reduce heat. Cover and simmer 10 minutes. Stir in butter beans. Cover and simmer 10 minutes. Sprinkle each serving with cheese.　10 SERVINGS.

Cut the potato into lengthwise strips, then chop strips finely.

Add chopped potato to ground beef, egg and bread crumbs.

Savory Meatball Soup

1½ pounds ground beef
  1 egg, slightly beaten
 ½ cup dry bread crumbs
  1 medium potato, finely chopped (about
     ½ cup)
  1 small onion, chopped (about ¼ cup)
 ¼ cup milk
  1 tablespoon snipped parsley
  1 teaspoon salt
  1 tablespoon vegetable oil
  1 can (28 ounces) whole tomatoes
  1 can (10½ ounces) condensed beef broth
  2 cups water
  2 medium carrots, sliced (about 1 cup)
  2 medium potatoes, cut into ½-inch pieces
     (about 1 cup)
  1 small stalk celery, chopped (about ¼ cup)
 ¼ cup snipped parsley
  1 envelope (about 1½ ounces) onion soup mix
 ½ teaspoon dried basil leaves
 ¼ teaspoon pepper
  1 bay leaf

34

Mix ground beef, egg, bread crumbs, chopped potato, onion, milk, 1 tablespoon parsley and the salt. Shape into 1½-inch balls. Cook meatballs in oil in Dutch oven until light brown. Remove meatballs; drain fat from Dutch oven.

Mix tomatoes (with liquid) and remaining ingredients in Dutch oven; break up tomatoes with fork. Heat to boiling; reduce heat. Cover and simmer 30 minutes, stirring occasionally. Add meatballs; cover and simmer 20 minutes.

8 SERVINGS.

Hearty Beef Chowder

1¾ cups hot water
 1 package (5.5 ounces) hash brown
    potatoes with onions
 2 tablespoons chopped onion
¼ cup butter or margarine
 1 tablespoon flour
 4 cups milk
 1 can (12 ounces) whole kernel corn with
    sweet peppers
 1 package (3½ ounces) dried beef, cut into
    1-inch pieces
½ teaspoon salt
½ teaspoon lemon pepper
¼ teaspoon celery salt

Pour water on potatoes; let stand 10 minutes. Cook and stir
onion in butter in 3-quart saucepan over medium heat until
light brown, about 2 minutes. Stir in flour; cook and stir 1
minute. Stir in milk gradually.

Drain potatoes; rinse. Stir potatoes, corn (with liquid),
dried beef, salt, lemon pepper and celery salt into milk
mixture. Heat to boiling; reduce heat. Simmer uncovered
until beef and vegetables are hot, about 2 minutes.
4 SERVINGS.

Dilly Pea Soup

1 pound split yellow peas (about 2¼ cups)
5 cups water
1 tablespoon vegetable oil
1 bay leaf
1 tablespoon salt
½-pound pork boneless shoulder, cut into
   ½-inch pieces
1 tablespoon dried dill weed
   About 2 cups water

Heat peas, 5 cups water, the oil, bay leaf and salt to boiling
in Dutch oven. Boil 2 minutes; reduce heat. Stir in pork
pieces and dill. Cover and simmer until peas are mushy,
about 1 hour.

Stir in about 2 cups water to desired consistency. Heat to
boiling, stirring occasionally.   7 SERVINGS (1 CUP EACH).

SPLIT PEAS are available year round and commonly used (with meat) in soups. They are high in incomplete protein and their nutritional value is enhanced when combined with meats or dairy foods. Soak before cooking as you would dried beans. Store at room temperature in a tightly covered container for 6 to 8 months.

Curried Pea Soup

1 pound green split peas (about 2¼ cups)
5½ cups water
1 cup chopped cooked ham (about 4 ounces)
2 teaspoons salt
1 teaspoon instant minced onion
1 teaspoon curry powder
1 cup water
½ cup cocktail peanuts
½ cup chutney
½ cup toasted coconut (see note)

Heat peas and 5½ cups water to boiling in Dutch oven. Boil 2 minutes; reduce heat. Stir in ham, salt, onion and curry powder. Cover and simmer until peas are mushy, about 1 hour.

Stir in 1 cup water. If necessary, add more water to desired consistency. (Soup will thicken as it stands.) Serve soup with side dishes of peanuts, chutney and toasted coconut. 8 SERVINGS.

Note: To toast coconut, spread on ungreased baking sheet and bake in 350° oven, stirring frequently, until golden brown, about 15 minutes.

S-T-R-E-E-T-C-H IT WITH PEANUTS!

Peanuts are such a rich source of protein that ⅓ cup can be substituted occasionally for a 2- to 3-ounce serving of meat. Provide a gallery of peanut garnishes and snacks for your family and watch the protein show.

Cook and stir carrots, onion slices and garlic in oil until the carrots are tender.

Stir in water, beans and seasonings; simmer 15 minutes. Add franks; heat 5 minutes.

Frank-Bean Soup

3 medium carrots, cut diagonally into slices
2 small onions, sliced
1 clove garlic, finely chopped
2 tablespoons vegetable oil
3 cups water
2 cans (15 ounces each) pinto beans
1 teaspoon salt
¾ teaspoon dried thyme leaves
　 Dash of Worcestershire sauce
10 skinless frankfurters, sliced

Cook and stir carrots, onions and garlic in oil in 3-quart saucepan over medium heat until carrots are tender, about 10 minutes. Stir in water, beans (with liquid) and seasonings. Heat to boiling; reduce heat. Simmer uncovered 15 minutes. Add frankfurters; heat 5 minutes.　　6 SERVINGS.

Baltic Picnic Soup

1 medium onion, chopped (about ½ cup)
2 tablespoons vegetable oil
4 cups water
3 medium carrots, thinly sliced (about 1½ cups)
2 medium stalks celery (with leaves), thinly sliced (about 1 cup)
2 teaspoons salt
½ teaspoon dried chervil leaves
½ teaspoon dried thyme leaves
2 medium zucchini, cut lengthwise in half, then into ¼-inch slices
1 pint cherry tomatoes, cut in half
1 pound Polish sausage, cut into ¼-inch slices
1 can (20 ounces) white kidney beans or 1 can (15 ounces) great northern beans

Cook and stir onion in oil in Dutch oven until tender. Stir in water, carrots, celery, salt, chervil and thyme. Heat to boiling; reduce heat. Cover and simmer until vegetables are tender, about 30 minutes.

Stir zucchini, tomatoes, sausage and beans (with liquid) into vegetables in Dutch oven. Heat to boiling; reduce heat. Cover and simmer 30 minutes. Skim fat if necessary.

6 TO 8 SERVINGS.

Cut frankfurters while the bacon and onions cook.

Prepare the bread while the bouillon dissolves.

Add beans and macaroni to soup while bread toasts.

Toast second side while the macaroni simmers.

Roman-Style Bean Soup

4 slices bacon, cut up
2 green onions (with tops), sliced (about
   ¼ cup)
1 can (16 ounces) stewed tomatoes
4 frankfurters, cut diagonally into slices
3 cups water
3 teaspoons instant chicken bouillon
⅛ teaspoon salt
⅛ teaspoon pepper
1 can (17 ounces) kidney beans
4 ounces uncooked shell macaroni (about
   1⅓ cups)
Garlic Toast (below)

Cook and stir bacon and onions in 3-quart saucepan over medium heat until onions are tender; drain. Stir in tomatoes, frankfurters, water, instant bouillon, salt and pepper. Heat to boiling; reduce heat. Cover and simmer until bouillon is dissolved, about 5 minutes.

Stir beans (with liquid) and macaroni into tomato mixture. Heat to boiling; reduce heat. Cover and simmer until macaroni is tender, about 10 minutes. Serve with Garlic Toast.   4 SERVINGS.

GARLIC TOAST

Heat oven to 400°. Spread butter or margarine, softened, over 1 side of each of 8 slices French bread. Sprinkle garlic powder and grated Parmesan cheese over butter. Bake on ungreased baking sheet until tops are golden brown, about 7 minutes. Turn slices; spread with butter and sprinkle with garlic powder and cheese. Bake 7 minutes longer.

Smoky Sausage-Bean Chowder

1 pound great northern beans (about 2½
  cups)
3 cloves garlic
1 bay leaf
1 tablespoon vegetable oil
5 cups water
1 can (10¾ ounces) condensed tomato soup
1 envelope (about 1½ ounces) onion soup
  mix
1 package (12 ounces) fully cooked smoked
  pork sausage links, cut into ¼-inch slices
½ cup water
⅛ teaspoon ground cloves

Place beans, garlic, bay leaf, oil and 5 cups water in Dutch
oven. Heat to boiling. Boil 2 minutes; remove from heat.
Cover and let stand 1 hour.

Heat beans to boiling; reduce heat. Cover and simmer until
beans are tender, about 1 hour.

Stir in remaining ingredients. Heat to boiling; reduce heat.
Simmer uncovered, stirring occasionally, about 10
minutes.   8 SERVINGS.

GARLIC, the aromatic
member of the onion family,
is a flavor staple. When
cloves are added to soups
and stews, they become as
mild as cooked onions. ¼
teaspoon garlic powder is
equal to 1 clove garlic.

Robust Chowder

1 can (10¾ ounces) condensed cream of
  chicken soup
1 can (8 ounces) stewed tomatoes
1 cup shredded Cheddar cheese (about 4
  ounces)
1 teaspoon dry mustard
8 frankfurters, sliced
1 can (16 ounces) sliced potatoes, drained
1 cup milk
2 medium stalks celery, sliced (about 1 cup)
1 can (8 ounces) sliced carrots, drained
1 can (8 ounces) lima beans, drained
1 tablespoon snipped chives

Mix soup, tomatoes, cheese and mustard in 3-quart saucepan. Stir in remaining ingredients except chives. Heat to
boiling; sprinkle with chives.   6 SERVINGS.

Chinese Chicken Noodle Soup

2½- to 3-pound broiler-fryer chicken, cut up
  1 teaspoon salt
    About 5 cups water
  2 cans (4 ounces each) mushroom stems
    and pieces (with liquid)
  6 green onions (with tops), finely chopped
    (about ¾ cup)
  2 large carrots, cut diagonally (about 1½
    cups)
  ¼ cup soy sauce
  1 tablespoon sugar
  1 tablespoon dry sherry
  1 teaspoon crushed gingerroot*
3½ ounces uncooked vermicelli

Heat chicken, salt and enough water to cover chicken to
boiling in Dutch oven; reduce heat. Cover and simmer
about 40 minutes.

Cool chicken and broth quickly. Remove chicken from broth; refrigerate broth. Remove skin and bones from chicken; cut chicken into bite-size pieces. Skim fat from broth.

Place chicken pieces, broth and remaining ingredients except vermicelli in Dutch oven. Heat to boiling; reduce heat. Simmer uncovered until carrots are crisp-tender, about 20 minutes; remove gingerroot. Stir in vermicelli. Simmer uncovered until vermicelli is tender, about 5 minutes.

10 SERVINGS.

* ½ teaspoon ground ginger can be substituted for the gingerroot.

Gingerroot, the source of spicy ground ginger, is now widely available in many stores.

Place slice of gingerroot between sheets of waxed paper. Crush with mallet.

To store, cover gingerroot with sherry; refrigerate it up to 6 months. Or wrap and freeze.

Suggested equivalent: 1 teaspoon crushed gingerroot for ½ teaspoon ground ginger.

Quick Chicken Chowder

1 can (10¾ ounces) condensed tomato soup
1 soup can milk
2 tablespoons instant minced onion
2 tablespoons dried green bell pepper
   flakes
1 tablespoon instant chicken bouillon
½ teaspoon instant minced garlic
¼ teaspoon lemon pepper
2 cans (5 ounces each) boned chicken,
   broken into chunks
1 can (16 ounces) lima beans
1 can (15 ounces) sliced or whole new
   potatoes, drained and chopped
1¼ cups cheese-flavored croutons

Heat soup, milk, onion, pepper flakes, instant bouillon, garlic and lemon pepper to boiling in 3-quart saucepan over low heat, stirring constantly. Stir in chicken, beans (with liquid) and potatoes. Heat to boiling, stirring occasionally. Garnish with croutons.   6 SERVINGS.

Stir the matzo meal mixture to make a soft dough.

Drop matzo balls into the simmering chicken broth.

Chicken Matzo Ball Soup

2 eggs, slightly beaten
2 tablespoons melted chicken fat, butter
   or margarine
½ cup matzo meal
1 teaspoon snipped parsley
½ teaspoon salt
   Dash of white pepper
1 to 2 tablespoons chicken broth or water
6 cups chicken broth
1 medium carrot, cut into 2x¼-inch strips

Mix eggs and chicken fat. Stir in matzo meal, parsley, salt, pepper and 1 to 2 tablespoons broth to make a soft dough. Cover and refrigerate at least 30 minutes.

Heat 6 cups broth and the carrot to boiling in 3-quart saucepan or Dutch oven; reduce heat. Shape matzo dough into 12 balls. (For easy shaping, dip hands in cold water from time to time.) Drop matzo balls into simmering broth. Cover and cook 30 to 40 minutes. 6 SERVINGS.

Hearty Fish Chowder

2 pounds frozen halibut or haddock fillets,
   thawed
3 cups water
4 medium potatoes, cut into ½-inch pieces
   (about 4 cups)
1 large onion, chopped (about 1 cup)
1 medium green pepper, chopped (about
   1 cup)
1 medium tomato, peeled and chopped
   (about ¾ cup)
1 cup half-and-half
1¾ teaspoons salt
¼ teaspoon pepper
⅓ cup shredded Cheddar cheese

Heat halibut fillets and water to boiling in Dutch oven;
reduce heat. Cover and simmer just until halibut flakes
easily with fork, 10 to 15 minutes. (Cooking time varies
according to thickness of halibut.) Remove halibut and
broth from Dutch oven. Flake or cut halibut into bite-size
pieces; reserve broth.

Simmer potatoes, onion and green pepper in 1 cup of the reserved broth just until potatoes are tender, about 15 minutes. Stir in remaining broth, the halibut, tomato, half-and-half, salt and pepper. Heat until chowder is hot. Sprinkle with cheese.   8 SERVINGS.

Heat halibut and water to boiling. Reduce heat; cover and simmer 10 to 15 minutes.

Remove halibut from Dutch oven; reserve broth. Flake or cut fish into bite-size pieces.

Simmer potatoes, onion and green pepper in 1 cup broth until potatoes are tender.

Stir in remaining broth, the halibut, tomato, half-and-half, salt and pepper.

Creole Shrimp Soup

1 pound frozen jumbo shrimp in the shell,
 cleaned and deveined
1 can (10¾ ounces) condensed chicken
 gumbo soup
1 can (8 ounces) stewed tomatoes
1 jar (2 ounces) sliced pimiento, drained
3 small onions, cut into fourths
2 cloves garlic, finely chopped
1 cup water
¼ cup uncooked regular rice
1 teaspoon salt
½ teaspoon dried basil leaves
1 bay leaf
 Dash of red pepper sauce

Heat all ingredients to boiling; reduce heat. Cover and
simmer until shrimp is tender and rice is done, 20 to 25
minutes. Garnish with parsley.   8 SERVINGS.

SHRIMPLY SCRUMPTIOUS

Delicious and protein laden, shrimp are low in
calories—only 100 calories per 3-ounce serving.
Raw shrimp (heads removed) are greenish or pink
and are sold by the pound, frozen or refrigerated.
1½ pounds raw shrimp will yield ¾ pound cooked
(about 2 cups). Cooked shrimp (shells removed)
are pink and are sold by the pound. Canned shrimp
can be used interchangeably with cooked shrimp.

To devein peeled shrimp, cut about ⅛ inch deep along outside curve of each shrimp.

Lift out the black sand vein with the point of the knife. Rinse under cold water.

Cook and stir cauliflower in butter over low heat until crisp-tender, about 6 minutes.

Stir in the water, cheese, half-and-half, instant bouillon and spices; heat to boiling.

Cauliflower-Cheese Soup

½ small head cauliflower, separated into
   flowerets and cut into ½-inch pieces
2 tablespoons butter or margarine
1¼ cups water
⅔ cup pasteurized process cheese spread
½ cup half-and-half
1 teaspoon instant chicken bouillon
   Dash of ground nutmeg
   Dash of ground allspice
⅓ cup dry white wine
½ small green pepper, finely chopped
   (about ¼ cup)
   Paprika

Cook and stir cauliflower in butter in 3-quart saucepan over low heat until crisp-tender, about 6 minutes.

Stir in water, cheese, half-and-half, instant bouillon, nutmeg and allspice. Heat to boiling over medium heat, stirring constantly. Stir in wine; heat about 2 minutes. Sprinkle green pepper and paprika over soup.   6 SERVINGS (ABOUT ⅔ CUP EACH).

Tomato-Beer Soup

Mix 6 cans (5½ ounces each) bloody Mary cocktail mix,* chilled, and 2 cans (12 ounces each) beer, chilled, just before serving. Serve with zucchini-stick stirrers.
7 SERVINGS (1 CUP EACH).

*1 or 2 cans (6 ounces each) tomato juice can be substituted for 1 or 2 cans of the bloody Mary mix.

Avocado Soup

1 unpared small cucumber, sliced
1 medium avocado, pared and sliced
½ small onion, sliced
1¼ cups buttermilk
1½ teaspoons lemon juice
½ teaspoon lemon pepper
¼ teaspoon salt
  Dash of red pepper sauce
  Cucumber slices
  Mayonnaise or salad dressing

Combine all ingredients except additional cucumber slices and mayonnaise in blender. Cover and blend on high speed until smooth, about 1 minute. Garnish with cucumber slices and mayonnaise.   6 SERVINGS (½ CUP EACH).

Shrimp Bisque

1 can (10¾ ounces) condensed cream of shrimp soup
1 cup tomato juice
2 cans (4½ ounces each) tiny shrimp, rinsed and drained
½ to ¾ teaspoon aromatic bitters

Mix soup, tomato juice and shrimp. Stir in bitters. Refrigerate 2 hours. Garnish with snipped parsley.   6 SERVINGS (¾ CUP EACH).

Dill Yogurt Cup

1 can (10¾ ounces) condensed tomato soup,
  chilled
1 carton (8 ounces) unflavored yogurt
¼ cup water
1 unpared medium cucumber, cut into thick
  slices
1 medium tomato, chopped (about ¾ cup)
1 teaspoon Worcestershire sauce
¼ teaspoon salt
¼ teaspoon dried dill weed

Place all ingredients in blender container. Cover and blend
on high speed until smooth, about 30 seconds. Serve over
ice.   6 SERVINGS (ABOUT ⅔ CUP EACH).

Curry Tomato Cup: Substitute ½ teaspoon curry powder
for the dried dill weed.

Cheese Soup

1 can (11 ounces) condensed Cheddar
  cheese soup
1 cup milk
1 cup ¼-inch cauliflowerets
1 cup frozen peas, thawed and drained
1 tablespoon chopped chilies, drained
¾ teaspoon salt
¼ teaspoon chili powder
4 medium tomatoes, coarsely chopped
1 cup shredded Swiss cheese (4 ounces)

Mix all ingredients except tomatoes and cheese. Cover
and refrigerate 2 hours. Pour into soup bowls; top with
tomatoes. Sprinkle with cheese.   8 SERVINGS (¾ CUP EACH).

Pea Pod-Lettuce Soup

Pea pods from 1 pound fresh peas (about
4 cups)
½ medium head lettuce, cut into bite-size
pieces (about 3 cups)
1 medium onion, cut into fourths
3 cups water
3 chicken bouillon cubes or 3 teaspoons
instant chicken bouillon
2 tablespoons butter or margarine
2 tablespoons flour
¼ teaspoon dried thyme leaves
¼ teaspoon salt
⅛ teaspoon pepper
½ cup milk

Rinse pea pods (reserve peas to use as desired). Heat pea
pods, lettuce, onion, water and bouillon cubes to boiling in
3-quart saucepan; reduce heat. Cover and simmer until
pods are tender, about 10 minutes.

58

Puree pea pod mixture in blender, small quantity at a time (according to blender directions). Press puree through fine sieve or cheesecloth to remove fibers.

Heat butter in saucepan until melted. Stir in flour, thyme, salt and pepper. Cook over low heat, stirring constantly, until mixture is smooth and bubbly; remove from heat. Stir in puree. Heat to boiling, stirring constantly. Boil and stir 1 minute. Stir in milk and heat 5 minutes. Soup can be refrigerated and served cold.   4 TO 6 SERVINGS.

Rinse the pea pods and place them in a 3-quart saucepan.

Cook pods, lettuce and onion until the pods are tender.

Puree small quantity of pod mixture at a time in blender.

Press puree through a fine sieve to remove the fibers.

Cut loaf lengthwise in half.

Spread with cheese mixture.

Cheese Bread

½ loaf (1-pound size) French bread
1 jar (5 ounces) pasteurized process sharp
    cheese spread
2 tablespoons butter or margarine, softened
    Sesame seed, poppy seed or freeze-dried
    chives

Heat oven to 350°. Cut loaf lengthwise in half. Mix cheese and butter; spread over cut surfaces of loaf. Sprinkle with sesame seed. Place on ungreased baking sheet. Bake until cheese is hot and bubbly, about 10 minutes. Cut into 2-inch pieces.　6 SERVINGS.

Savory Bread

½ loaf (1-pound size) French bread
¼ cup Italian salad dressing
¼ teaspoon dried oregano leaves
½ cup shredded pizza or mozzarella cheese
  Paprika

Heat oven to 425°. Cut bread lengthwise in half; brush cut surfaces with salad dressing. Sprinkle with oregano, cheese and paprika. Bake on ungreased baking sheet 10 minutes. Cut into 1-inch slices.   6 SERVINGS.

Cobblestone Loaf

Place 1 loaf (1 pound) frozen bread dough in greased 9-inch pie plate. Brush loaf with vegetable oil. Cover and thaw up to 12 hours in refrigerator or 3 hours at room temperature.

Heat oven to 375°. Shape dough into round loaf. Snip top of loaf with kitchen scissors to resemble cobblestones as pictured. Brush with 2 tablespoons butter or margarine, melted, and sprinkle with ¼ teaspoon onion or garlic salt. Bake until golden brown, about 40 minutes. Serve warm.

Snip loaf with kitchen scissors to resemble cobblestones.

Brush loaf with melted butter; sprinkle with onion salt.

Parmesan Rounds

Cut ½ pound French bread into ¼-inch slices. Brush slices on both sides with ½ cup butter or margarine, melted; place on ungreased baking sheet. Set oven control to broil and/or 550°. Broil slices 4 to 5 inches from heat until golden brown, about 30 seconds; turn and sprinkle with about ½ cup grated Parmesan cheese. Broil until golden, about 30 seconds.   28 TO 30 SLICES.

Garlic Rounds: Substitute garlic salt for the grated Parmesan cheese.

Garlic Loaf

**1 package (about 1 ounce) garlic salad
   dressing mix
¾ cup butter or margarine, softened
½ cup shredded Cheddar cheese
1 loaf (1 pound) French bread**

Heat oven to 325°. Blend salad dressing mix, butter and cheese. Cut bread into ¾-inch slices; spread butter mixture over both sides of slices. Reassemble loaf; wrap in aluminum foil. Bake 30 minutes.   ABOUT 28 SLICES BREAD.

Spread mixture of salad dressing mix, butter and cheese over the bread slices.

Reassemble loaf (in 2 parts if necessary). Wrap securely in aluminum foil; bake.

Place the onion slices on the buttered bun halves.

Spread onions with the mayonnaise-cheese mixture.

Onion Buns

---

   4 **pumpernickel buns**
      Soft butter or margarine
   1 **large sweet onion, cut into 8 slices**
   ½ **cup mayonnaise or salad dressing**
   2 **tablespoons grated Parmesan cheese**

Cut buns in half and butter each half. Place onion slice on each half. Mix mayonnaise and cheese; spread over onions. Set oven control to broil and/or 550°. Broil 4 to 5 inches from heat until hot and bubbly, 2 to 3 minutes.
4 SERVINGS.

Butterflakes

Heat oven to 325°. Separate 12 ready-to-serve butterflake dinner rolls into individual sections; spread with ½ cup butter or margarine, softened, and ⅓ cup orange marmalade. Bake on ungreased baking sheet until golden brown, 10 to 15 minutes.   6 TO 9 SERVINGS.

Biscuit Squares

        ½ cup shortening
        2 cups all-purpose flour*
    1½ teaspoons baking powder
        1 teaspoon salt
        ½ teaspoon baking soda
        ⅔ cup buttermilk or sweet milk
        ¼ cup butter or margarine, melted

Heat oven to 450°. Cut shortening into flour, baking powder, salt and baking soda until particles are size of small peas. Stir in buttermilk.

Gather dough into a ball. Knead lightly 10 to 15 times. Roll dough into rectangle, 16x8 inches, on lightly floured cloth-covered board; brush with half of the butter. Fold rectangle crosswise in half; brush with remaining butter. Cut into 2-inch squares. Place on ungreased baking sheet. Bake until golden brown, 10 to 12 minutes.   16 SQUARES.

*If using self-rising flour, omit baking powder, salt and baking soda.

A
B
C
D
E
F